SLOAN-KETTERING

ℰ SLOAN-KETTERING
Poems

ABBA KOVNER

Translated from the Hebrew by Eddie Levenston

Foreword by Leon Wieseltier

Schocken Books, New York

All rights reserved under International and Pan-American Copyright
Conventions. Published in the United States by Schocken Books, a
division of Random House, Inc., New York, and simultaneously in
Canada by Random House of Canada Limited, Toronto. Distributed
by Pantheon Books, a division of Random House, Inc., New York.
Originally published in the Hebrew language by Hakibbutz
Hameuchad Publishing House Ltd., Bnei Brak, Israel, in 1987.
Copyright © 1987 by the author and
Hakibbutz Hameuchad Publishing House Ltd.

Schocken and colophon are registered trademarks
of Random House, Inc.
The poem "Detached Verses" was originally published in
The New Yorker magazine.

A Cataloging-in-Publication record has been established for *Sloan-
Kettering* by the Library of Congress.

ISBN: 0-8052-4198-1

www.schocken.com

Book design by Johanna S. Roebas

Printed in the United States of America
First Edition
2   4   6   8   9   7   5   3   1

For Vitka

About those days
when you were blond and radiant,
pulling the wool over German eyes,
like an imp   of mischief,
we assumed we would tell the
     children
while they were still children,
jointly;

about the pure madness
of the sane, the homeless,
without country, with no
     protection.
without even the color of your hair,
we thought to tell the grand-
     children
when they grew up, jointly;

who shall recount the valor of your silence
on that one day,   of more weight
than all the days
at Sloan-Kettering,   outside
the operating theater
when each one said in his heart
Live!
behind the screen,   meeting his fate
apart.

                                        3.14.1987

CONTENTS

FOREWORD

—In memory of Dr. William G. Cahan

It is an ancient complaint against ordinary life that it is erected upon a neglect of death, upon an evasion of mortality. Duty, custom, distraction, routine: all conspire in a general thoughtlessness about the evil that awaits every existence in its final disappearance from the world. We are pleased to turn our eyes away from the necessity of dying, even at the cost of living more shallowly. Perhaps it is the impossibility of remaining indifferent to death that requires of us our elaborate improvisations of indifference: were we to see death plain, we would see nothing else, we would be stilled by fascination and fear, we would stop and live only according to what reason soberly rules, with an intensity of consciousness that would disqualify us from common tasks and common pleasures, and shatter our passions, and transform our lives into solemn preparations for a lucid release. We would live deliberately and skinlesssly. We would be heroes, and philosophers, and saints, and monsters. But most people do not wish to be those things, and their reluctance to live grimly must not be scorned as a reluctance to live truthfully. They are not fools. They know that they will die, but they do not know it at every moment, and it is not all that they know. For the knowledge of life is not the same as the knowledge of death. In this one reality many things are real. The end is not all that is conspicuous. If there is dignity in living up to Socrates and Seneca, there is dignity also in letting Socrates and Seneca down.

But this vexation about how much death to let in to life is itself the evidence of a benevolent fortune. We forget about death because we *can* forget about it, because our circumstances permit us to forget about it. Our forgetfulness may be no more than a respite from the truth about our transience, but the duration of this respite may be long, and a great deal may be accomplished and enjoyed on its ground. Yet there are other sorts of circumstances, other sorts of existences. If there are individuals who need to be made mindful of death, there are also individuals who need to be made mindful of everything that is not death. There are people who have been condemned, by nature or by history, to live in proximity to death; who find it wherever they look, because it is to be found wherever they look; who must turn their gaze not toward their mortality but away from it, because otherwise its hectoring presence will always be with them. Abba Kovner was one of those people, one of doom's intimates. The most prominent feature of the universe into which he was born was the feature of extinction. In his time and his place, there was no way to experience life except as survival.

Kovner was one of the most valiant men in Jewish history, one of the most valiant men in modern history. He was a genuinely epic figure. He was born in 1918 in Sebastopol and grew up in Vilna, a young Zionist and a young sculptor. In 1941, after the Lithuanian capital fell to Hitler's troops and the Einsatzgruppen began their work, Kovner grasped, with precocious despair, that the massacres of Vilna's Jews represented nothing less than the first signs of a plan to exterminate all the Jews of Europe, and he promptly organized the first Jewish resistance to the Nazis. It was he who famously exhorted his brothers and sisters in the Vilna ghetto that they "not go like sheep to the slaughter." He took up arms in the ghetto, and then he took up arms in the forests. In 1947 to 1949, he fought in Palestine, some of which became, as a consequence of the sustained exertions of many magnificent wills like his own, Israel. He settled on a kibbutz and became a writer, and his ferocious poetry of witness immediately took its place among the literary treasures of the Jewish people. He died in 1987, after a struggle with throat cancer.

Kovner made literature out of that struggle, too. He came to New York for treatment at Memorial Sloan-Kettering Cancer Center, that great fortress of hot science and cold sweat; and this extraordinarily powerful book of poems—in the Hebrew original it is presented as a *poema*, or a single extended composition in verse—is the account of what happened to his body and to his soul during this, his final war. Kovner writes of his "journey into speechlessness," and not only because his surgeons removed his vocal cords. *Sloan-Kettering* shivers with the special beauty of a last work. The poet-patient dwells on his sharp sensation of corridors: the hospital itself is a corridor that cuts across life the way a highway cuts across the land and arrives at the sea, and in the background of these spiritualized logistics is the old rabbinical adage that life is itself a corridor, and so "prepare yourself in the corridor so that you may enter the banquet hall." These are poems of transit by a man who has no history of rest.

What prepares Kovner for his battle in Sloan-Kettering is not the anticipation of peace, but the recollection of war. These poems owe their force in part to the delirium of memory in which they were written. This book is the record of a haunting. "No! to the knife/ A second time," the poet exclaims as he waits for surgery. "You shudder like one/ challenged to stand up for his right to live," he remarks about a visit from his doctor. As his wife sits beside him in his hospital room knitting a sweater, the rhythm of the moving needles reminds him of "sounds that live within a man/ with all the other unrealities/ not wiped out/ in the massacres." The new dread returns Kovner to the old dread. He recalls Christmas eve in 1941, when he left the Benedictine convent that had given him sanctuary and trudged, a hunted man, through the snows back to Vilna, so as to establish the United Partisans Organization. "When leading a band of harried fighters/ or standing face-to-face with the enemy," he recalls under the influence of drugs, "holding out in the siege/ and standing alone/ on the ramparts,/ he never said that death is to be preferred, that life is negotiable."

These associations would be outrageous in any man for whom they were not real. But it was not history that the mortally ill poet was summoning in Sloan-Kettering, it was biography. There is nothing morbid about Kovner's metaphors of enormity, nothing cheap about his confusion of nature's threat to his life with history's threat to his life. He was fortifying himself with the resources that a hostile world had bred in him. He was using what he had, like all fighters do. And he was careful to note that he was no more than "half-drugged" in the hospital: these were not hallucinations, these were reminiscences, and before their facticity the reader must bow his head. Was Kovner's imagination disproportionate? But his experience was disproportionate. "Not one of the things he valued came to him easily." He had not cheated death; life had cheated him.

Yet the author of these poems has no pity for himself. Indeed, he is perfectly aware of the difference between cancer and genocide, and of the varieties of human desperation. He sleeps propped up against his pillows, "trying to hold/ in memory/ worse things/ in order to tell his pains/ they were not worth anything/ they should leave him alone for now." Remembering the forest in the hospital, he admonishes himself: "do not waste/ your despair/ in all kinds/ of waiting rooms." In the most delicate lines of his book, Kovner writes: "Soon/ soon we shall know/ if we have learned to accept that the stars/ do not go out when we die." It is an exquisite moment of severity with himself, a rare warning against the vanity of the survivor. Sometimes, it must be admitted, Kovner made too much of defiance as a prescription for living; but he was not exaggerating when he described himself, in a poem about discovering in the morning that his blanket was wet from the night, as "a man who had fought the world." We teach what we have learned. The happy man is as partial in his comprehension of the world as the unhappy man. The most extreme suffering, too, is just a point of regard.

Adorno once observed that "in the face of death one cannot cut a powerful figure." That is the typical error of the true materialist. It is certainly the case that nature, unlike history, leaves no survivors; but we are not only natural beings. We may master fear and we may aspire to glory. If we may not gain immortality, we may still gain posterity. We are finite, but we are not slaves of finitude. Regard the example of Abba Kovner. When he died, death was proud.

—Leon Wieseltier

❧ 1. Introduction

And like that
the door opened without a click
pushing aside the shifting straw curtain
his shadow entered
followed by the man with his mane
of dark hair
a young man with
large eyes

At once
they took their places at the head of his bed
(the shadow quietly folded itself away
between the sink and the bedpans)
and with the stance of a Trappist-to-be
he declared: "The time has come."
"My time has come?" he trembled.
"That's what I said," he added
like a professional phantom.
"Where are we going, do you really know the way?"
"We are taking you there." He fell silent.

"Can I ask a question?"
"Too late."

(The swine!) "Let me take a towel,
some soap, a book?"
"Unnecessary. Anyone who enters
comes out as he went in."

At once he turned
to leave. As he went out,
trailing after him came his smell, his shadow
and his dread.

᥍ II. THE CORRIDOR

HE FELL ASLEEP UNDER STRANGE SKIES

He fell asleep under strange skies.
Vaulted windows
                    the neo-renaissance style
of New York Hospital.   Outside
the last thing his eyes took in
clearly:
three chimneys   a crematorium
a red-tiled roof   at the back
Rockefeller University,
the medical center,
a world of vanished routines,
your home and your rooms suddenly emptied
of yesterday's light.

STILL INSIDE

East River
beyond the foot of the wall. Like
a crimson tongue silently   encompassing
Roosevelt Island   the river
gently ripples.
Shocked by the sight of power soaring above him
concrete
and dark glass
proud gods—
ready to forgo the knowledge acquired
to cope with self-examination, studying
the powers

                                        assembled
                          summoned up and recruited
                                    to cut throats

still inside. Outside
a small finger fumbles for
that bag of skin and bones,
to say through dry lips:
No! to the knife.
A second time.

FICTION CAUGHT IN THE THICKET

Dr. Strong is a large-limbed man,
a surgeon brimming with confidence. When he talks
about cancer of the throat, the head or,
let's say, the larynx,
chasms melt away. But when he draws near
the edge of the bed and looms
over your face, your heart falls
before the cold blue of his eyes,
an indifferent patch of sky,
and you shudder like one
challenged to stand up for his right
to live, even with closed eyes;

a second. Another
half second—and after
nine hours of anesthesia,
when you return and open them,
and speech rises and is heard
floating out of the darkness,
a still, small voice,
you know a little more about the nature   of the heart

and the world and the man
whose hands have done everything for you
that a man's hands can do

and the rest is with heaven - - - -

SLOAN-KETTERING

Sloan-Kettering (its full name: Memorial
Sloan-Kettering Cancer Center)
is a large and growing building
and all those who come within its walls
to strip
naked,
jointly and separately,
suddenly find themselves
in a cage, captive, exposed

and the silence astounds on all
its many floors
and when a patient
cut off from his supervisor
finds himself running
from room to room
with no idea where to turn
first, peering down the glaring corridors,
half-open doors and half-
shut,
Sloan-Kettering is a personal encounter

with a pathless wilderness
between yellow arrows
and blue signs
something obscure is going on
in the feverish cells
of your brain
at the entrance to a triple elevator
that has not yet
opened its maw
like a desert
beginning to take shape

from within;

TRANSPARENT INFUSION

Drop
by drop
colorless atropine
oozing down
into his veins,
like death. Like his name spelled out
in a foreign language

dripping from every telephone receiver
and receiving an American reply
to soothe the foreign breast
                        You are welcome, sir.
Doesn't cost a cent. He marvels:
the fingers of the black nurse on duty
are like the velvet pads where Mother
kept   her needles
a sweet velvet pad like
chocolate—

She looks at him but sees nothing:
>Your pulse is fine, sir.
Thank you.
You're welcome.

His prayer stand

Is there a prayer for one who prays like him
seething. He has offered no sacrifice, built
no altar. He has not grasped the coattail
of a flying angel,
nor placed his trust in the mercy of heaven;

is there a prayer for one who prays like him
seething. Once he loved the lonely
dweller in the sky. He remembers
the day he lost patience waiting
for the echo of his cry for help
to come back from empty space.

His prayer stand now
is the nickel clothes hanger
above his bag of bones wrapped
in a chilly sheet as he prays
before bottles hovering

like acrobats on trampolines—
is everything liquid? Is there nothing
solid—
after the infusion?

GLADIOLI, A FERN

Gladioli,
a fern
    and roses that burst open yesterday.
The wealth of flowers from Interflora assuage
the cold whiteness of the walls,
the appalling silence
of the infusion tubes
waiting
beside his starched bed: the emergency light,
the suspended switch and the thoughts
trembling fearfully
above the foul enfeebled body.

Which makes the presence
of his son's face here so strange, Nimrod and Amikam
visible in colored Polaroid above the night table—
Amik has a sad expression—
of childhood that doesn't know the reason.
Michael—brimming with joy and beauty

leaning over the tulip
heads
in Talpiot.

In their presence
in their presence
may one cry?

Beyond the screen

Beyond the screen lies a man from Thailand,
in anguish, wheezing as he breathes
into a plastic sleeve.
                          Unless our geography is wrong,
in origin he is Siamese, from a country of free people
once;
              you don't have to peep behind the screen
to see the remnants of the old man's family
as he spits phlegm into a plastic bag,
life supports sitting around him.
                                        Like the cities we have built so
      proudly,
how wretched is their splendor in the presence
of those who live on, in solitude, in their dead world.
                                                  Lost parchment
in the heart of the desert, his yellow a faded gray,
the Thai stretched here, spitting phlegm
into a plastic sleeve, while the soft steps
of his wife, his son and his daughter-in-law,
running past him, bringing glimmerings of life
that return, like an image ungrasped,

swallowed up in the core,
in the arms of an octopus,
the largest of the cities of cold
stone.

Infuriating confidence

The infuriating confidence of the doctors
at the Memorial Center
holds something of the mystery of
the Jerusalem hills.
—You are no more than transient visitors!
say the hills of Jerusalem.
Move on.
Move on
as far as
the frontier
right there!
A dangerous bend
—slow down!
Slow down,
you have been warned!

Go in. Come out.
One step farther
—keep moving.
There's nothing worse

than a corridor in the middle of
laughter—
farther. Farther!
Along the Trans-Israel Highway.
Sloan-Kettering is
a trans-life corridor.

CRAZY TAMMUZ

A crazy Tammuz turns metropolitan New York
into a place of exile, lying in front of me like a ball of fire,
haze and heat wave.
                Clouds and rain
                                asphalt
evaporating with a smell of corruption
from the mouth of the drugged earth—
                                in New York
there is everything—bridges and buildings,
commerce and crime—and they exaggerate
the scale of it all,
for New York contains itself
and much more.

Only Gabriel Preil, a short balding Jew,
with a pure face and soul, contains just himself.
He still writes poems in Hebrew and Yiddish,
plants sunflowers at the side of the road
sees
trucks going down the freeway.

23

THERE AND BACK

On his first trip to New York
New York was New York
so many things from New York
passed before his eyes
he never tired of looking more
and more—

on his last trip to New York
New York was a never-ending
hospital and of the things that
passed before his eyes
his eyes saw
nothing

and since he knew so well
what to expect, his mind
wandered round and round
New York

and far from there and from anything
still familiar

like a path in the desert
stricken blind
—Will he never return to a decent life?
—Has he no right to die
while still alive?

OPPOSITE THE STATUE OF LIBERTY

That day she was truly magnificent,
the lady holding the torch aloft.
The nation was enjoying itself on both sides,
both sides of the Hudson, ours
and the other

letting their hair down with millions of sparks
too grown-up to be embarrassed
by childish pranks

          launching
collapsible boats upon the waters
all in operatic naval costumes
after more than a hundred years
of freedom purchased with fireworks

—twenty tons of fireworks!

O God of Abraham, Isaac and Jacob,
give us a handful of fireworks

for the next twenty years
and we shall return to thy city Jerusalem
with a full heart
after serious operations.

✎ III. ROOMS

WHEN THEY TOLD HIM

When they told him they were going to cut away his vocal
    cords
entirely it was merely
a confirmation of what he already knew
and it sat deep inside him like a dark lump
but the certainty that that very evening
he would awake dumb—
and the sophisticated shiny white bed
that you could raise and lower and split
in two, head one way
and feet the other,
the bed and the hanging bottles,
the Puerto Rican nurse, Norma,
the ceiling and all the tall, wide windows
of Sloan-Kettering swept by
and faced with
untidy papers
with no print
with no print
dark
his spirit fails. The stone

that carried to his throat the lump
of tears that would not burst—
his lips moved. Dr. Strong did not understand,
nor did Dr. Chu, only Norma the Puerto Rican girl
whose almond eyes clouded over as though
she heard a familiar dirge.
He was singing:
Oyfn pripetchik brent a faierl
un in shtub iz heis
un der rebe lernt kleyne kinderlekh
dem alef-beis . . .
How many years of his life he would have been ready to give
in exchange for a good ear
and a sweet voice! But he was always out of tune:
the more he loved something,
the worse he made it sound,
orphaned melodies

. . . suddenly his hearing sharpened. On trembling
lips the tune died away
with no great protest. The remaining
words streamed to his throat
to be uttered with the last sound of his voice
what he wanted to tell you
and they fled
like the land unfolding in panic

beneath the speeding railway carriage
(Budapest–Graz, remember?).
The inner fear.
The inner dread.
The inner rage and
the innermost awareness
that he can no longer escape
this confrontation
and when he lifts his arms from the infusion
this one
and this
in silent prayer
perhaps he will see the voices again
in the empty East River landscape
and rediscover the light of your face

within.

THE WINDOWS GROW DARK

The windows grow dark
and the grim snort
rasping from the next bed
never lets up, makes the night shudder.

He begs for his life. Prays
for an hour's sleep. And the croak
emerging from the depths of the body on fire
billows up the paths of prayer
en route for heaven.

He never asked his name. By chance
they met near the operating theater.
When they awoke on the same breathing wave
of faint hope under the oxygen
masks, they seemed to have known each other
since early childhood,
and in the darkness of the windows, as though
trapped in a building going up in flames,
they sought each other
and the emergency exit.

And their eyes did not fill with tears
but with waves like the tide
coming in
covering the dips in the sand. For him, too,
everything returned to normal
apart from the peace beyond sleep.

HIS BLANKET IS STILL WET

His blanket is still wet from the night.
How he longed for the night to end.
To extricate his bare feet
from sinking in the gooey bog
of another life:

                        naked they are placed
on scales   one   then another
to weigh their chance of remaining alive.
The hand of a young nurse—
for a thousand two hundred days he has known
no one like her—holding his arm.
Supporting his hips, without noticing
touching what had been his privates and without
embarrassment continuing to talk about him
as though talking   about ancient shards—
they could not understand how such a skeleton
could still remain alive.
They could not imagine that this was a man
who had fought the world,

body
and soul,
it was not he who had given life a name
of such fatuity—

                    his blanket is still wet from the night.
Until the duty nurse arrives,

he will reclaim his bare feet
from the place into which he has now declined,
revive his frozen toes,
stroke his heels, feel
the dividing line between
a body feeble but alive
and a swamp that smells of death.

WHAT HIS SOUL ADORED, AND HATED

What his soul adored,
and hated.
When Norma puts out the lights
behind his closed eyelids
that fire blazes.
He hears flames consuming
the pocketknife he received
from his girlfriend at his bar-mitzvah,
the Shabbat candlesticks, all the door
handles
cast from strange metals,
the portrait bust
in his own likeness
that he didn't want.
The rest of the copper was of course requisitioned
by the Germans, though the Poles came first,
for the war effort. It didn't help
either of them. He remained
without the knife
given him by his first girlfriend,
who believed he would be a great artist

carving in walnut, mulberry,
a true likeness
before he had an image of his own
that he didn't want
and didn't like.

TASHLIKH

And he threw
the abyss at you   like an extinguished
lime pit
in his eyes
                    and he rejected
your conciliatory hand
in fury
and as he passed across the sky
from one side to the other
he could not find
a smile for you
or reprieve
for himself
only when he began to understand
to be aware
that in a place abandoned
by innocence
by dream
there is nothing to be found
but an abyss,
perishing.

TOUCHING THE BROW,
TOUCHING A MELODY

Moving aside the ice pack
your fingertips lightly
touched his brow
deer stood erect in the lilac light
behind the standing corn
coming away from the sun
close now
his fingertips touch
their silky skin
he leaps in their tracks over
the hilltops—
how could you know
that as your hand touched
his feverish brow
he shook off the wings
of the cold angel
and went off singing with the deer
plucking a melody for them
on the hilltops---

RECOVERY

He leaned his forehead against her shoulder.
Yielded his mind to his heart.
Conquered half the fears
of a man going to embrace
his fate
and digging his nails
into her forearm
allowed his eyes to shed
wild longings in the hot
burst of tears
of a babe redeemed
from the hands of its captors.

LIKE A SEAL

1.
How little we need
to be happy:

a half-kilo increase in weight,
two circuits of the corridors
at Sloan-Kettering
in bedroom slippers
a morning without aspirin
silence gentle as a pit,
a distant
sand dune
behind the green bridge
a patch of lawn
and you beside me beginning
to knit a new sweater.

2.
The rhythmic movement
of the needles between your fingers
has something of the beat—ai-li

43

lu-lu-li—
sounds that live within a man
with all the other unrealities
not wiped out
in the massacres.

LIQUIDS SEEK A WAY OUT,
AND SO DOES HE

Imagine him sleeping
in a sitting position propped up
against a heap of pillows
his head elevated
as much as his neck, stiffened
by eight thousand units of radiation,
would allow him to keep it, as high
as required in order not
to suffocate
trying to hold
in memory
worse things
in order to tell his pains
they were not worth anything
they should leave him alone
for now—

listening to the silence in the rooms.
A Jew to his fingertips
cannot exist

45

without meaning
without probing to the end
of this sudden muteness
perhaps absence of speech
also has meaning
beyond the physical fact
that it is not the whole
of existence—Rise above it! Who
is urging him tonight?—
Rise above the nettle-infested
wall—with broken fingernails,
grasp at the darkness
as though it holds the eyes
of a survivor.

Imagine him thus
asleep
and
awake.

Before the CT

Not yet sunset. Until the cloud shadow
falls across the aluminum ceiling
from a different angle,
his head and most of his body will remain
under the CT.
                    This elegant cave
will scan his secret places
in less than an hour
with uncompromising assurance.
                    In the mountains of Palmyra,
when they set up the most advanced of radio-
telescopes, the planners rejoiced
like young goats
it was now within their power to scan
the uttermost secrets
of the universe—
today we know the universe is so constructed
that its uttermost ends flee and escape
far beyond the visual grasp
of the most advanced radio-telescope,

beyond space—
isn't that how cancer sits,
microscopically,
lurking in his vocal cords
hiding from the eyes of the doctor
concealed from the self-assured rays
of the CT?
An abyss fine as a pinhead
in ambush,
with mysterious patience
like the galaxies of emptiness
beyond the black holes
left behind in space
like a fateful seal
with no dawn—

alone with his thoughts,
his musings,
his muse
sings—
the sun somewhere above him (at home
he could be more precise)—your hand!
Lay the palm of your hand
on his fevered brow. Let us not be
like two hills staring

at each other
in the grim light
of the setting sun.

CONSOLATION

It will not last. A few more weeks,
a month, two at the most,
the wounds will heal.
Everything will get better.
Apart from what is no longer there.

IV. HALF-DRUGGED

NINE O'CLOCK. NORMA

Nine o'clock. Norma brings a pill to sweeten his sleep
if you can say sweet dreams on a night of strain,
exhausted by a wild dream that recurs
with minor changes, like caressing
the stern of a foul-smelling ship
that brought them to safety on the dockside
before the harbor was sealed off at two in the morning.
The whole night full of caresses. He stood caressing
the soggy photo of his grandchildren, then
his palms stroked each other,
the wind grew stronger, frost and vexing snow. He sings.
Works at singing.
And the stones that tore the flesh of his hands and feet.
The jagged surface
of the large stones in the land of his fathers
and he knew full well there is no land of one's fathers
without people, so he ran
feet and hands moving over the stones
battered in every part of his body, screaming
from pain and pleasure,
for his scarred tissue was lapped

by waves of salt water
and he screamed mightily
and only the sudden appearance of the Puerto Rican nurse
who stood between the doorway and the screen,
embarrassing,
unreal, asking,
"Did you ring the emergency bell, sir?"
obliged him to ask: "What time is it?"

UNDER THE SKIN

Every morning at a fixed time he had an appointment
with an injection. Every night took him back
to the life that was, beyond the distance
and regret. You ask him: "Will we ever
get out of this terrible forest?"
And without blinking an eyelid he says: "We will, my dear,
in a year's time we will be out."
Michael, too, did not tell his parents until
long long after that he had been
in Beirut with the planes. I alone
tell my mother everything I do not dare to reveal
to my diary. At the end of every night I sit
and tell her about fears, imprisonment, an unclosed
account, sometimes about
the grandchildren. She should have a little joy
in Ponar. At the time when
the novocaine is decomposing,
dead times are decomposing,
looking for a way out from under the skin
like lymph
after surgery.

VISITING TIME IS OVER

Visiting time is over. Now
without pretense
in the long corridor
directionless
alone
another
circuit
and another
with no voice.
Then whence the insistent
voice: Be strong,
hold on!
For what purpose
in the final reckoning?
Norma, black Puerto Rican
nurse, how many years
have you been cleaning
the filth
of others?

The visiting hour he yearned for
has passed,
the night he dreads
has come.

DEATH IS NOT TO BE PREFERRED

When leading a band of harried fighters
or standing face-to-face with the enemy,
holding out in the siege
and standing alone
on the ramparts,
he never said death is to be preferred,
that life is negotiable;
anxious
frightened
by severe privations
he never asked anything
of Almighty God
but to grant him favor
and ease his pain
when he leads the congregation
in communal prayer:
and forgive our sins
in love
and joy
and gladness

and peace
O God,
Mighty
and Awesome.

CONTACT WITH STEAM FROM
THE INHALER AND THE WATCHING EYE

Steam gathered you into the railway carriage.
The station at Milan teemed with people—
the only ones who seemed natural among the motley throng
were your bodyguards
three loyal followers
short men wearing
the uniform of the Jewish Brigade.
P. had not forgotten to bring some Belgian chocolate
with that old-time flavor.
Shaike, so you told me later, stroked your hair
which had recovered its peroxide fairness
as they wished you bon voyage, praying
with mixed feelings;
but none of them had any idea
that the following day you would be under arrest
at the frontier post,
in the toilet chewing
your forged documents
your blood racing
like sand marking the last hours

between devastation and the promised land.
Meanwhile the nurse in green had managed
to repair the tube of the inhaler;
the steam that had escaped from undesirable places
had dissipated
along with you
and the steam in the railway station
and Milan
so
far
away!
But an oath! If your admirers had been aware
of the level of wickedness
to which they descended
in addressing you
there
as our sister!
Saying with genuine passion:
Poor thing, how will you be tomorrow
without your grief,
without the wreckage of your life!

Going to meet his brothers

The day he left the convent
on Christmas Eve
the shelter and its approaches
the wall and the gate
all
the paths were covered with
snow
every moment the storm waxed
every moment he had to tramp through
bigger and bigger piles
whipped up by a howling
whistling
whirlwind
and still he trudged
plodded
burrowing
finding a way through
gasping for breath
impatient
though still the snow was not deep enough
to be really dangerous to those

used to walking, day in day out,
in snow
but he was a young townsman stranded
between town and convent
totally unused
to walking
in the snow
in the infamous chill
of winter 1941.

And he walked on through the snow, looking round
as one pursued
for in those days there was no lack
of keen-eyed hunters
even in a storm
even in the snow
even on Christmas
Eve.

So every halt was dangerous
in the stumbling
progress
of the young townsman

very non-Aryan

•   •   •

he slowed down for a barking dog
for an old farmer
greeting them with a blessing
for the holy day
almost kneeling
before a wooden Jesus
at the green bridge
after all he had gone out bareheaded
into the storm
and he didn't care very much
if for the sake of appearances
he did kneel down
once more
going to meet his brothers.

THE WOMAN KNITTING
AND THE SPIRITS

Ash-gray
veins covered the back of your hand
coming under the dull green
bedside light of the recovery room
it wrapped them in a transparent
silken glow
without raising an eyebrow (that, too, hurt)
he could see how
your hand gathered up his sighs
like stitches fallen from the knitting needle
one
by one
suppressed
fading away
between your warm fingers
—pick up a stitch!
—pick up a stitch!
Above his scarred neck hovers
your shadow—

It is rare for history to record
such a state of total identification
between two close souls
abandoned to their fate
each one now weeping
on the point of a different
                              indicator
Silence!
Silence!

I don't know, he told them, how
you have the heart
to come to me with the sorrows
of a world that is past. After all, you no longer
are grieved by death
nor by the departure
of the Divine Presence.
            "The flowers appear in the land,
            the time of the singing-bird has come."
And will you feed me, he said to them,
on dust
for all the remaining years
of my life?
They said: Even a dead man needs some days
of joy. A home he can visit
without prior notice, otherwise

what do we have to do in your world?
they said.
It's not fair! he shouted.
It's not fair. Gentlemen!
You don't write prayers over
the body of a man
alive.

VIOLENT INTERRUPTION

Before his eyes
steeply they fall
and rise
again
words without context;
they are holocaust survivors, you said,
they emerged stricken in body
and soul.
After what happened to them
we must be careful. They said:
The worst of all comes back.
They did not extinguish the fire.
They have not lit the light.
One day, damn it, one
fine day it has to stop!
But they had such a penetrating
smell—

in the ghetto the lice
got under your skin. The story of the ghetto
did not get under your

skin. When, my friend,
did you last visit
the likeness of the questioner,
the other one
inside you, flesh of your battered
flesh
to ask him, black brother, your morning coffee
that smelled of smoke—what did it taste like?
And another question.
And another
for it is not the answers that are important. Only
by questions is man empowered. And no final summary,
just no rounding off,
in the name of God!

ʚ৹ V. HONORED VISITORS

TODAY IS THE SIXTEENTH OF JULY

In memory of Itzik Wittenburg

Today is the sixteenth of July?
On the sixteenth of July
forty-three years ago,
on the night before the sixteenth of July,
they raced trembling between the walls
at daybreak
                     on the sixteenth of July
which never ends
he shouted to them:
You madmen—

Get down!
Get down!
The total reckoning.
Yearning for the dawn:
Get down!
Get down!

One thousand ten thousand
to the gate
now!
On the dawnless night
of the sixteenth of July
a wretched horde is ready
to eat you alive—

Forty-three years!
The gate is still open. The wicket
and the sound of his footsteps on the cats' heads
slowly slowly
a nation holding its breath
and at that moment he passes over
to the other side—

A shoemaker, his name forgotten, who did not know
that his son, too, was in the underground, blows his nose
not on his apron, and says: Remember
what day it is today! Happy the people
that has such sons—

for forty-three years
on the night of the sixteenth of July
he has been turning in his bed

his weeping unrecorded

                              Was it in vain
the sixteenth of July   or the final sacrifice
of a-people-who-always-miss-their-chance?

She, to him

1.
I am the wind that did not abate
I shall break through your window
to encircle your face;

weeping is forbidden.
Weeping is forbidden.

Only touching your blood
with the edge of a wing.
I am unseen
and prohibited to you;

2.
I filled your secret to overflowing:
longing for dawn,
longing for night.
Longing for laughter.

How could you travel such long
distances without me?

3.

Flying by night. With one stroke
crossing the vast skies, oh my dear!
Traveling all the way only to confirm
that the distances are internal.

4.

I could tell them that my face was pressed
against the window of the airplane
digging tunnels to the edge of the sky
all through the night.
I could have told them that arriving early,
being by your side for one hour, would give me
one more day of life.

5.

They never learned to love. They will not pray like me
for childhood to be restored
free from fear, without forbidden things.
Imagine, suspecting me of glorying
In your suffering.

6.

Weeping is forbidden.
Black sobs congeal in my throat.
Along with my tears

I shed my desires. My love. Avi.
And will this sever the cord? Is this
the flaming sword of our maturity?

7.
In vain we strove to understand
whether we had broken through
or I was leaving captivity like
a baby learning to walk.

In vain you strove to understand
whether freedom rejoices in my eyes or
a reflection of the abyss remains ungrasped in them.

Do not examine who I am
now. With no regrets;
at present,
my birth—your life.

It makes no difference what they caught,
the town police.
To hell with what they will say,
the village idiots.

8.

Our love was torment. Nothing
seems clearer than to call
a rose a rose and our story
love. It is something else
to carry wordlessly
the blaze of love

one more step
into the abyss.

Could you have prevented me from calling you Avi?
Did you not know by what name I called you,
speaking to myself?
Seeing nothing but
my prayer. My fear.

Our tragedy is so stark;
I shall never find the strength
to banish you from my terror.
My beloved on the far side! When I am awake
you never cease
to sing my dream.

XENOPHON AMONG THE
JEWISH PARTISANS

I.

And then they searched for lice by the outskirts of the fire
and roasted potatoes for the evening meal
in the embers
and brewed tea with green swamp water
with toads watching the show.
Every man sitting with his gun. They pass the night
in burrowed earthen dugouts, well camouflaged,
young men and women together,
no rape here, just making love,
for the earth is cold in Lithuania and the winter is hard.
And Russian partisans come from afar
lusting after Jewish girls. For the fame
of Jewish girls has spread throughout the forest
and the Jewish partisans had a war on their hands
in the front and at the rear.

2.

And Cyrus fell in the battle of Kunaxa. And they cut off
his head and his right hand. And the head and right hand
of Imke were hanging with his entrails on the electric fence,
which had been torn apart by the explosion.
They brought the body of Danko, Imke's brother, last night
from where he had fallen on the other side of the river,
and Imke was not yet eighteen,
he never waged this war and his young man's feet
did not step on the mine
in order to conquer the kingdom of Persia.

3.

Like the men of Sparta, you never heard partisans
weep. But as they finished interring
two young brothers,
the last of their family line,
you could take explicit note
of the wail rising from the pine trees
from branches weighed down
with so much snow.

4.

Without Xenophon. Neither Imke
nor Danko is here. He alone

circulates among trees smelling
of novocaine,
trying to place himself in a proper relationship
with . . . my God!
To wake up mute
in a strange bed

         and without the fear of the forest.

AND NIMROD CRIED ALOUD

Jerusalem has no sea
and jellyfish have no jaws, but all night
Nimrod cried aloud:
Jellyfish!
Mommy, jellyfish!
with fear in his eyes. And Leivick
is buried three stations away
and no one visits his grave
like they visit Père Lachaise.
Père Lachaise upset him;
and who does he have, and who
is left in a New York of millions
of Jews after Leivick?
But Père Lachaise is in Paris. And Paris
flows in the veins. What does history do
when learned in young veins: and he followed her
from Saint-Denis to the Place des Vosges
and also saw her jingling
from a distance of two fingers
but to himself and in Hebrew he said aloud
that his eyes were not drawn to her panties

only to Victor Hugo's mean, empty house
in the Place des Vosges. Tourists, *les misérables*,
hardly visit.
He left there alone
as though wrapped in a chilly shroud,
breathing chloroform.

A HEALTHY RECOVERY

—What a healthy recovery,
they said. And patted him on the shoulder
with admiration: You're doing fine. Wow!
More than expected. Someone even went so far
as to say: A miracle!
He sleeps peacefully,
our boy, he has even put on weight.
But he remembers days
when they abandoned us like orphans.
When they came back from starvation,
he and his comrades, they had no problem
putting on weight. Sometimes the milk
served so plentifully in the dining hall
was rose pink, but this was an illusion, just
the refraction of distant light
in colored windows—
and with what speed they recovered
from the horror and the memory
talking about comrades who had fallen
one by one before their eyes
and their eyes did not fill with tears

but with waves like the tide
coming in,
covering the dips in the sand. For him, too,
everything returned to normal
apart from the peace beyond sleep.

PERHAPS WE HAVE
NO BETTER EVIDENCE

Perhaps we have no better evidence for God
than his seeing us. In a thousand bonds
linking creature and Creator
he is committed to life—
since that night, like the night
of burnings, when he lay down
in a snow-swept dog kennel
preserving the image
of G-d;

the same man

is old now, sick with cancer,
with no Sabbath free from harsh
memories. His door is open
to slightly
crazy
visitors

(now) Norma comes in

from another world,
her nocturnal bosom bursting out
of her white uniform,

he smiles at her, embarrassed
like a little boy
who has wet the bed, but very little,
since most of it (what joy!) went straight
into the bottle. He blushes
when Norma says: What a lovely
head of hair you have, sir!
Respectfully she transfers the needle
from vein to vein
without unnecessary anguish
                              before she goes,
thank God.
                        From now till dawn
he will have another visitor.

INDEPENDENCE

I gave you a mad life. I gave you
a home. I made for your home
a bell
garden,
rightfully yours,
so that coming
going
there would be reason
to praise—
you would have someone
to curse,
someone to betray,
whenever and without fear,
you would be able to inflict on him
your bitterness!

I gave you
a mad life
so that you would not lack,
God forbid,
a day of thanksgiving

full
filled with all the goodness
of the Land
so that you would not forget
your protector;
                    the giver of life,
your loneliness.

∾ VI. AN EXERCISE WITH SLIPS OF PAPER

(slips of paper as a limited experiment in writing a will)

If we could lift one more veil
we might reveal
the face of our near ones
more than the things
for which we went
to war

INSCRIPTIONS

1.

Not one of the things he valued
came to him easily.

2.

Let what remains of what he wrote
stay in the archives
it is not for the operating table.

3.

A burden of molten
rocks.

4.

Later he turned his mind
to finding leisure
for something that was not work
and without clarification
not a mission.

5.
Shame on you:
outside there was a sixth
war.

6.
And thus he learned
that what comes easily
goes easily

7.
These are the dreams.
Apart from the one that was no
bother while he was awake
until

8.
Yitgadal veyitkadash

9.
The house of his father
and his mother
by herself:
in front of her the Sabbath
candles

it happened last Friday
when his arms were already connected to the tubes
and fit for nothing
except to cover his face.

10.
shemei rabba;

11.
He held himself tight, leaning
his head. He did not cry. As though
resting,
he didn't want the nurse to think he had fainted,
his mother to suspect,
God forbid, he had no shelter
for his head.

12.
Who screamed? He
himself (how?) or a stranger
(who?)
three dogs after him
in the middle of the empty
market
no one there

just him in his shirt
(with the dogs sniffing at his crutch)
he did not call this horror
fate—
green spittle dribbled from his lips
onto the green bridge
—Mother!
—Mother!
he screamed soundlessly.

LIKE AN ACCOUNTANT

Self-examination. Turning the pages
over and over
morning and evening
sometimes in the middle of the night
like an anxious accountant
but not very strong, neither at spiritual
accounting nor any other
kind. He tries to distinguish
between credit
and debit
page
by page
but in the last analysis, what does it matter!
Life—if he could,
what he would like to tell you is this:
life what is left of it
is hard to give up
hard
even now.

From waiting rooms and beyond

When he was in the forest,
a man of the forest,
he lit fires there.
When he built himself a home
he wanted a fireside
in place of an "eternal light."
Imagine how he hated
waiting rooms
this man with his face
to the future:
with their arms folded;
legs crossed
alternately,
knitting needles let fall
for lack of patience;
the gnawed fingernails of
a woman at the dangerous age;
the extinguished pipe of the man
with the mask of self-confidence;
and all in an atmosphere
of slow death—

My friends! How much he wanted to say
to you then from the bottom of his heart:
Whatever happens, flee—
get out!
Where to? Doesn't matter, just as long
as you can still rekindle
the forgotten fire
in the heart of the forest—
provided only that you do not waste
your despair
in all kinds
of waiting rooms.

Be strong and . . .

From heaven came no mercy on *Shabbat "Bereshit"*
at 09.00 from the wreckage of his voice
there arose a bubble
a tiny bubble
pa
pu
like a glass shattering at the bottom
of a ruined well
and from the well came an answer . . .

                             Thus

he began his journey into speechlessness.
He said to himself, Look
in the name of heaven! This is not
the end of the world.
And his common sense added: Far worse
were the things you have already seen,
by God!
And from his guts
he heard a voice saying:
Remain what you were!
Remain what you were!

three times.
And he still tried
to make himself laugh, saying:
You've talked enough, man,
in your lifetime—
and when he felt his lips bitten

                              till they bled

by the time the blood
had become nothing
like other blood
nothing at all
he said
with the sound of a hollow tree:
Okay then!
Let's return to the world
from a pile of cotton wool.

B-918

He left Room B-918 behind him
clean,
tidy, after packing the books
that were beginning to be a burden
he gathered up the slips of paper and pencils
blunted
by so much accumulated bitterness
by lack of ability to express himself appropriately
he closed the narrow closet, handed in
the key to the hospital office
shifted the night-light
to the corner of the table
where he found it on arrival, closed
the shutters on the window
only the wound remained open
and the mirror empty,
a white restfulness.

ᥫᩣ VII. Landing

HE STOOD THERE

When the gates of the hospital opened before him
and he went out into the street free
to go on his way, he stood there by the hospital gates
wondering whether to hail a taxi or to keep
walking, going out not coming in.

The avenue was already decorated for
Christmas, bathed in fluorescent light, a feat
of color, and the city lay open before him in all
directions and he wondered which way,
going out not coming in.

On the corner of Sixty-eighth Street, right opposite
the hospital, a Korean was selling all kinds
of novelties from his stall, including
masks at ninety cents each, and he stood there
wondering, going out
not coming in.

And when the policewoman blew her whistle,
to his surprise it sounded like the scream of a bird

shot by mistake, and he just turned his head
sideways and covered
half his face with a scarf
of wool.

                        Wool is not good, he thought,
it burns the skin, which is swollen like
the skin of a drum! And here he covered
his disfigurement with a splayed hand, striding
for the heart of the powerful wave that flowed
up the avenue bathed in lights, twinkling
for Christmas: Keep walking!
Keep walking! he said with locked
throat, in front of
the red
traffic light.

AND THERE WAS NO IMPEDIMENT
TO HIS PRAYER

And there was no impediment to his prayer.
There were impediments every day
at 06:15
in the morning
and at 11
mid-morning
and at 1 p.m.
and at 01:00
and in the middle of the night
in the middle of the night
whenever his hand gripped
the emergency bell
the wheezy pump
the bed-
(where is it, for God's sake!)
pan
every day when he set out
and came back
from the long corridor
(with yellow arrows)

everything substantial
that he held in his hand
every day
he asked for
one
more day
no longer to be

"of modest achievement . . ."
"And the righteous / and the saintly / and the pure in
    heart . . ."
kept their distance
heard nothing
saw nothing
only the corners
of their lips
only the movement
of their beards
of their
(may there be no impediment to)
prayer;

FEARFUL FROM THE MOMENT
OF ARRIVAL

Fearful from the moment of arrival: he
watches the landing that cannot
be avoided, into
the arms
of people who love him, waiting
a long while already
a long while in fine
irritating
rain, like the strangled breath
of a shower,
they saw him tap the window
of the plane like
the wing of a trapped bird—
someone said

it had started already
when the plane began to lose
height with the fastenyourseatbeltsplease
and then suddenly and against
all reason and all—

the stars also came down
to land a thunderous blow
and there was flame from the exhaust
even then he was frightened by the expected
pilgrimage to the gate
of his rejuvenated home
surrounded by good friends
waiting with the patience of friends
for what he would say,
which would not be heard,
and the conversations that would erupt
on all sides
as though straining to fill the empty space
and the television is congested
it glows like an eternal light
and the intervening silences fall
like a blunt ax
since you
and only you
were the one called upon
to banish the memory of a desperate flight
from sleepless nights
harder
than stones

• • •

trying again
to escape the dead
before sunrise—
looking at his surroundings. Looking
at those who remained. Here.
Who had not fled from anywhere, stayed
here, felt at home.
Business as usual.
No one changed his habits, weekdays
or holidays. Not one of the questions
was asked, not one
forgotten, not a single ten o'clock cup of coffee
neglected.
There is a time to sow. And a time to reap.
Conversations more persistent
than before
burning up the last drop of moisture
from your lips
as though between blazing shutters
and were they also then
were they also then
as they stood dying on their feet
were men brothers here
united
in bread, butter and games?

Not on the operating table
in the alien whiteness of Sloan-Kettering Memorial Hospital
but here above this ground
before dawn. At the moment of arrival
as the wheels touched
down:
trembling on the verge of the heart
rising and taking a position
like a barefoot traveler—
such is fear. And he knew
where and when
the wound opened.

And since he knew so well
what to expect, his mind
wandered round and round
New York
and far from there and from anything
still familiar
like a path in the desert, stricken
blind
—Will he never return to a decent life?
—Has he no right to die
while still alive?

ON HIS RETURN

On his return he found his home restored
to his liking
so neat and tidy:
the garden like two lungs breathing
a welcome
with the brown troughs of geraniums
and the wealth of flowerpots
on the tiny veranda
adorned
by the midday sun
watered with love. Idit

worked hard for three days removing
the dust from the shelves
of books
old friends
winking at him
even friendlier
than before, no change of dress,
they too keep their distance
from embarrassment and/or

some obscure fear
and everything in its place. Familiar
and arranged the way he had asked for
long ago. Only
the sun in his spectacles,
the sun like glass
shattered against his eyes,
why does he see the sun
through different eyes?

ONE LIVING WORD

No more willful silences.
No more verbal contact,
he who loved to listen to so many
will never again hear his own voice among them.

He will sit with his friends over talk
from now on under constraint.
The talk. The thoughts. The friends.
And as he listens through
the secret door
he will turn his inner ear
to the dark murmur: Son of man,
all this
and all this
never was
and never will be
as good as
one living word.

Nothing new

Five or six times I rang you,
no answer. Either you're out a lot
or occupied most of the time
or the telephone company, God damn it,
is to blame as usual.
I wanted to tell you that with me
it's business as usual. I'm back from New York
after some tough therapy. Apart from that
there's nothing much new. Ronit has gone back to work
after the seven days of mourning. Her friends consoled her,
her Boria was a lucky man—
to die over a game of chess. It's almost
marvelous. Ronit, as we know, is an actress
from way back. This time she is wearing no mask.
Her daughters took very good care of her
throughout the period of mourning, now they've gone home,
one to the South, the second to Galilee,
Hagit has moved to Tel Aviv.
That's the way it goes. Ronit, too, has joined
the widows' club. Like Bruria,
ten years already. Her son-in-law, so they say,

is achieving great things in the factory
and has increased the turnover from two to twenty-five
million. Although I understand nothing
about output, I understand
that this is wonderful. Tomorrow Gershon
starts chemotherapy. Anat and Eli
have gotten divorced. Hantze will now have a problem
at teatime on Shabbat.
We had the grandchildren for Hanukkah. I didn't
sing "*Ma'oz Tsur*" with them, you know why.
Malka (thirty-one years a widow) fusses around me
as though I were a child. Her fourth grandson
is completing recruit service. She is baking a cake—
I'm sure there's a lovely smell coming from her oven,
but I'm quite unaware. Several
of my senses vanished after the operation,
but I'll tell you about that and about
other things some other time,
if there is one.
P.S.
There will not be
another conversation. Just as this one is no more
than the invention of a throat in ruins.

Detached verses

1.
Soon
soon you will pass from the darkened room
to another world. Freed from debts
and contacts.

2.
One more
one more look
at the neighbor's garden
and his dog asleep
on the still warm tiles.

3.
A headline
a headline still blaring
by the base of an overflowing garbage can.

4.
A little
a little longer in the setting light of
the sun.

5.
The stub of a moment of parting
from things we ignored when we could still
live erect on our feet.

6.
Things we believed would never
fade have already been abandoned
by your memory.

7.
If only you had been one of the philosophers!
Giving a flavor of meaning
to ruined buildings, to acts
of heroism, to our fate.

8.
Was that leap
into the depths
any easier?

9.
Soon
soon we shall know
if we have learned to accept that the stars
do not go out when we die.

THE WHOLE ACCOUNT

You began to love in times of disgust.
Close at hand there was no tree, no sign
of a living stem or flower, and when there was no reason to
　　sing
it was your laughter, jubilant, rousing, saying: There is
　　someone here
alive—joyful! And many, so many, then were lying curled up
　　and fearful
in grimy shadow, and you began to love without dousing the
　　light of the carbide
and went down to the boat that threatened to break up at
　　sea, and you conceived
against doctor's orders. Unannounced, you strode the dead
　　streets,
marching—all forty-five kilos of you!—as if on a victory
　　parade
of life flowing beneath the surface of all
the words, like a fountain flowing, cascading
with confidence, telling no lies.

LIKE A COMPUTER SCREEN, LIKE LIFE

You had no need to make an effort
to avoid pretense.
You did not pretend,
laughing or crying,
for forty-three years.
Wedded to his bed,
your face was as legible
as words on a computer screen, clear and sure.
His wretched, irksome needs,
the dough of his distorted lineaments,
each sign, each life-giving gesture
you recorded like a phosphorescent graph
without pause, morning
and evening.
                    Never give up!
For him and for yourself, no frost
only the rising sun—
it's hard not to sound sentimental, but that is how
it is preserved in a man's memory,
only the potter's clay

not a nude exhibit, not
a computer screen
but the genuine
fact of life.

AN ENDING, UNFINISHED

Where now?
he asked himself that Thursday morning
when in silence they left the office
of the department head.

Where now—
he was still thinking to himself. But
it would have been hasty and impolite
to make difficulties for everybody present,

there were five of them. He and his wife
went out, the three doctors remained behind
to finish their business.

Where now—
actually, who did he want to ask?
The trees that graced the central lawn
rustled gently. Something metallic
like tin or lead pressed on his pensive
brain;
without bitterness. And without bearing any grudge

against anyone in particular, he let his eyes scan
the taxis clustered about
the main entrance to the building,
like words assembled for handprinting
by an obsolete process—

                            Where now?
It's not yet noon
even. And a cloud has begun slowly, slowly,
to cover the sun
he missed so much when abroad.

Notes on the Text

The following notes are translated—and sometimes expanded—from those supplied by Dan Miron in his Hebrew edition of the third volume of the *Collected Poems of Abba Kovner*. (Those notes that would not be necessary for readers of the English translation have been omitted.)

STILL INSIDE   Lines 20–21: No! to the knife.
                                A second time.
"*Oystrekn dem haldz tsum messer / Nayn! A kaynmal nayn!*" (To hold out the throat to the knife? No! Forever no!) Quoted from a poem that was sung in the ghetto by members of the underground, a way of swearing to fight for one's life.

FICTION CAUGHT IN THE THICKET   The language in the title echoes the biblical account of the binding of Isaac in Genesis 22:13.

TRANSPARENT INFUSION   Line 3: atropine
A painkilling drug (also known as belladonna).

HIS PRAYER STAND   The title—"*ken tefilotav*"—is a punning reference to the phrase "*qen tefilotai*" (my nest of prayers) in the well-known poem "Hakhniseni Tahat Knafekh" by Haim Nahman Bialik (1873–1934).

GLADIOLI, A FERN   Line 14: Nimrod and Amikam
Abba Kovner's grandchildren by his eldest son, Michael, who is referred to in line 18.

CRAZY TAMMUZ   Tammuz is the fourth month of the Hebrew calendar, corresponding to June. The Yiddish expression *"meshuggeh fun Tammuz,"* a Tammuz lunatic, means a man whose lunacy is seasonal, occurring in the hot season.
Line 14: Gabriel Preil
A Hebrew poet (1911–1993) who lived in New York for most of his life.

THERE AND BACK   The final lines of this poem are repeated word for word at the end of the poem "Fearful from the moment of arrival." By direct repetition the poet suggests the degree to which such thoughts obsessed him throughout the Sloan-Kettering experience. He uses the same device in the poems "The windows grow dark" and "A healthy recovery," which end with the same six lines.

OPPOSITE THE STATUE OF LIBERTY   Lines 4–5:
"both sides of the Hudson, ours
and the other"
An allusion to the Hebrew poem by Zev Jabotinsky (1880–1940), which speaks of "the two banks of the Jordan, ours and the other."

WHEN THEY TOLD HIM   Lines 28–32:
Oyfn pripetchik brent a faierl
un in shtub iz heis

un der rebe lernt kleyne kinderlekh
dem alef-bais . . .

This is a well-known Yiddish song, *"Oyfn Pripetchik,"* by Mark Warszawsky: "A little fire burns in the hearth, and the room is warm, and the rabbi teaches little children the alphabet."

Line 48: Budapest–Graz

A reference to the many journeys made by Abba Kovner when he was serving with the Brikha, the underground movement for transporting Jewish refugees to Palestine during the years that followed the end of World War II; tens of thousands of Jews, packed into railway carriages, made their way from Central Europe to the Mediterranean ports. On one of the journeys from Budapest to Graz, there was nearly a disaster; Kovner, who was sitting on top of one of the carriages, fell off and was almost killed.

THE WINDOWS GROW DARK   See note to "There and back."

"TASHLIKH"   The title literally means "You will hurl": it is the name of a ritual of absolution from sin, performed near running water after afternoon prayers on the first day of Rosh Hashana, the New Year, when the final verses of the book of Micah are repeated—"You will hurl all our sins into the depths of the sea."

UNDER THE SKIN   Line 8: Michael

Abba Kovner's eldest son served in an elite unit of the Israel Defense Forces.

Line 16: Ponar

A wood on the outskirts of Vilna. "On the 5th of April, 1943, four thousand Jews from the surrounding villages were packed into

83 carriages and transported to Ponar, where they were all shot," as Abba Kovner wrote in his essay "Testimony—A First Attempt." (*On the Narrow Bridge*: Sifriyat Hapoalim, 1981, p. 15).

THE WOMAN KNITTING AND THE SPIRITS   Lines 36–37:
"The flowers appear in the land,
the time of the singing-bird has come."
Quoted from the Song of Songs 2:12.

HONORED VISITORS   The section title here is the Aramaic word *ushpizin*, or holy guests, a name for the souls of Abraham, Isaac, Jacob, Joseph, Moses, Aaron and David, who, according to Kabbalistic tradition, come to visit every pious Jew in his *succah* during the festival of *Succot*.

TODAY IS THE SIXTEENTH OF JULY   On July 16, 1943, Itzik Wittenburg, the commander of the underground forces in the Vilna ghetto, handed himself over to the Gestapo in order to save the other members of the ghetto from collective punishment.
    Line 26: cats' heads
    A term for the smooth cobblestones with which the streets of towns in Eastern Europe were paved.

SHE, TO HIM   The Hebrew title of this poem, literally translated, means "Breaches, a direct flight." It has been changed in order to clarify what is clear from Hebrew grammar but would otherwise remain obscure in English translation: that Abba Kovner ("Avi") is the addressee and the speaker is a woman—probably a dear friend of his from before he married Vitka, who then became "prohibited" to him.

"Avi" is an intimate form of the first name "Abba" and also means "my father."

XENOPHON AMONG THE JEWISH PARTISANS   Xenophon is the author of the *Anabasis*, an account of his journey with an army of ten thousand Greek soldiers across Asia Minor to the Black Sea.
Line 16: Kunaxa
The site of the battle where Cyrus the Younger was killed.

AND NIMROD CRIED ALOUD   Line 6: Leivick
H. Levik (1888–1962), a well-known Yiddish poet and playwright, author of the poetic drama "The Golem." He is buried in a cemetery near New York.
Line 9: Père Lachaise
A well-known cemetery in eastern Paris—named after the Jesuit priest François Lachaise, the "father confessor" of Louis XIV (1624–1709)—where many prominent figures from literature, music and the theater are buried.

INSCRIPTIONS   Stanza 3: molten/rocks
This phrase is also the title of a volume of short stories, published in 1945 by the Hebrew writer Hayyim Hazaz.
Stanza 8: *Yitgadal veyitkadsh*
The first two words of Kaddish, the mourner's prayer.
Stanza 10: *Shemei raba*
The second two words of Kaddish.

BE STRONG AND . . .   The title is an allusion to the exhortation "Be strong and of good courage." See Joshua 1:6.
Line 1: *Shabbat "Bereshit"*

The Sabbath on which the annual cycle of reading the Pentateuch is begun with the first chapter of Genesis. *Bereshit* is the Hebrew word for "in the beginning."

HE STOOD THERE The title alludes to Psalm 122:2: "Our feet stood inside your gates, O Jerusalem."

AND THERE WAS NO IMPEDIMENT TO HIS PRAYER An allusion to the cantor's prayer ("and may there be no impediment to my prayer") in the *Prayer Book for the New Year*, given to all patients by the hospital rabbi in New York just before the New Year. The phrases "of modest achievement" and "And the righteous / and the saintly / and the pure in heart" are quoted from the same prayer.

ABOUT THE AUTHOR

Abba Kovner was born in 1918 in Sebastopol. Committed to Zionism from boyhood, Kovner was an advocate of armed resistance during World War II, famously urging his comrades in the Vilna ghetto not to go "like sheep to the slaughter," but to stand and fight. Kovner thus became a key leader in the United Partisan Organization, which carried out sabotage operations against the German army, first from the ghetto and later from the Baltic forest. After liberation, he helped to take Jews from Eastern and Central Europe into Palestine for resettlement. Kovner and his wife, Vitka, also a resistance leader, eventually settled on Kibbutz Ein ha-Horesh. After taking part in the Israeli War of Independence in 1948, Kovner became a writer of both poetry and prose, winning the Israeli Prize for Literature in 1970. A founder of the Moreshet Holocaust Institute and the Diaspora Museum in Tel Aviv, he died in 1987.

About the Translator

Eddie Levenston was born in London in 1925. He taught applied linguistics, including the theory and practice of translation, at the Hebrew University of Jerusalem, where he worked from 1958 to 1991. His translation of Yoel Hoffmann's *The Christ of Fish* won a prize from the British Comparative Literature Association in 1995 for Best Translation of a Work of Jewish Interest. He has also translated Abba Kovner's book on the Holocaust, *Scrolls of Testimony*. He lives in Jerusalem.

A NOTE ABOUT THE TYPE

The text of this book was set in Van Dijck, a modern revival of a typeface attributed to the Dutch master punchcutter Christoffel van Dyck, c. 1606–69. The revival was produced by the Monotype Corporation in 1937–38 with the assistance, and perhaps over the objection, of the Dutch typographer Jan van Krimpen. Never in wide use, Monotype Van Dijck nonetheless has the familiar and comfortable qualities of the types of William Caslon who used the original Van Dijck as the model for his famous type.